How to Move by Bike:
Tales and tips to inspire

Dear Damian,

THANK YOU so very much
for helping to kickstart this
book. Hope you enjoy it.
You're wonderful!

Sincerely,

STEPH

How to Move by Bike: Tales and tips to inspire.

Hopscotch Town Publishing, October, 2013
www.hopscotchtown.com

Cover art: Shawn Granton
Interior Illustrations: Ethan Jewett, Ted Buehler,
and Steph Routh
Typesetting: Brad Reber

Contributing Authors: Aaron, Babs Adamski,
Audrey Addison, Kristin Bott, Ted Buehler, Mike
Cobb, Steve Couche, Kristi Joy Falkowski, Erinne
Goodell, Shawn Granton, Josh Guttmacher, Beth
Hamon, Esther Harlow, Amos Hunter, Heather
Anna Jackson, Ethan Jewett, Lily Karabaic, Scott
Lieuallen, Chris McCraw, Noel Mickelberry, Becky
Morton, Kirk Paulsen, Matt Picio, Katie Proctor,
Ron Richings, Maria Schur, Brian Scrivener, and
Halley Weaver.

Edited and designed by Steph Routh

First printing, October 2013
ISBN 978-0-9910855-0-7

Printed in the United States of America by
1984 Printing on post-consumer paper with
soy-based ink and animal-free binding

10 9 8 7 6 5 4 3 2 1

dedication

To my parents, who have inspired love of the bike and been incredibly supportive of even the weirder aspects of my multi-modal love affairs (to wit: my father walked me down the aisle when I married my Schwinn in 2006).

I love you. You rock.

CONTRIBUTORS

Aaron
Audrey Addison
Zed Bailey
Kristin Bott
Ted Buehler
Mike Cobb
Steve Couche
Kristi Joy Falkowski
Erinne Goodell
Pat + Geoff Gordon
Shawn Granton
Josh Guttmacher
Beth Hamon
Esther Harlow
Amos Hunter
Heather Anna Jackson
Ethan Jewett
Lily Karabaic
Scott Lieuallen

Chris McCrow
Noel Mickelberry
Becky Morton
Kirk Paulsen
Matt Picio
Katie Proctor
Tomas Quinones
Brad Reber
Ron Richings
Maria Schur
Brian Scrivener
Halley Weaver

Why MOVE by BIKE?

Need to move to a new house or apartment but hate renting the truck and the process of packing and unpacking? Boy, have I got a solution for you: move by bike. Moving by bike is a dearly-loved event for those who have taken part. It's a great, cheap, and strangely quick alternative to renting a motorized behemoth and begging a few friends to help you do all the work.

There are, understandably, skeptics of the amazing potential of the bike move. It can be difficult to understand just how brilliant and fun bike moving is until one partakes of the magic.

Doubter McSkeptic: How could it possibly be quick?
Bike Moverson: We don't have to wait for the teensy, congesting bottleneck of the rental truck door.
Doubter McSkeptic: But what about that one hill?
Bike Moverson: That hill has to end somewhere.
Doubter McSkeptic: That would be a lot of furniture.
Bike Moverson: Bring it on!
Doubter McSkeptic: But how can you possibly move something as big as my mattress?
Bike Moverson: Are you kidding me?

Moving by bike is like a barn-raising for the urban environment, a gangly parade that migrates the innards of one's living room from hither to thither, all to the melodious sounds of bike bells and friendly calls of "car up!" People have moved a puppet theatre, a few small businesses, file drawers, a chinchilla, more than one hide-a-bed, countless bookcases and chests of drawers, pianos, accordions, plants, a gun safe, saplings, and a documentary crew, to name just a few items. You don't need a trailer, just moxie and a sense of fun and adventure.

As of this printing, I've done fifty-eight bike moves (two mine, 56 other people's), and I believe there's no finer pastime than joining a bicycle caravan of someone else's belongings, and pedaling down residential streets with a gaggle of others. Children erupt from their houses and call for their parents to come and look at the amazing parade of stuff. Drivers - who would otherwise be pissed at the few seconds' delay - elbow their passengers and jockey for their cameras. Poor unfortunate souls who have succumbed to the rental truck move follow the bike move with their eyes and sigh.

More than a fun and easy way to jump the drudgery of moving, bike moves remind us of what is possible.

And, if you were wondering, no we didn't get the idea to move by bike from "Portlandia." They got it from us. That is the last we shall speak of it.

forklifts and rototillers

aaron

My first bike move was actually from the train station to a temporary residence. I have always been carfree and didn't know how I would get all of my stuff hauled away from the train station. Someone on the Shift email list lent me a 'Bikes at Work' trailer, and using it changed my life.

Toughest load

I hauled a 300+ pound rototiller from SE Portland to S. Milwuakie. The only real difficulty was getting it loaded, as it was too heavy for me to lift. With a neighbor's help, we got it on my trailer, and I just rode slowly down the flattest roads I knew all the way.

The strangest thing

A manual forklift that was used for raising several enormously heavy beams at a construction site (it weighed over 300 lbs). I loaded it on my trailer and took it back to the rental company on the east side of Mt. Tabor.

Favorite story

My favorite would have to be Matt Picio's epic bike move from south of Clackamas Town Center all the way along the Springwater and up to Ladd's addition. Because there were several places where bollard placements made for a narrow constriction, we took measurements of the maximum width that we could load as well as the height of the bollards. Anything that was too wide had to be loaded on top of other items to raise it high enough to clear. Some pieces cleared with barely an inch of space.

a bike move love story
heather anna jackson

I saw a video about it on BikePortland while living in Atlanta, so I decided I wanted to live in a city where this sort of thing happened. On my first bike move 7 years ago, I met many folks who are still close friends.

I met my husband, Jim, at Jeff and Jill Cropp's Move by Bike on a hot September day. He showed up on a tandem with my friend Adam. Super fox. I nearly fell over. I later described him to friends as a combination of David Duchovny and Dennis Quaid. He was wearing a snug white t-shirt and shorts, and I couldn't stop staring at the back of his neck and legs. But I thought he was a stoner.

While we picked tomatoes from the Cropp's front yard, he kept picking green tomatoes and eating them, then gagging. He asked me how to tell which ones were ripe. I said don't eat the green ones (thinking, "Really?"). After the bike move, I invited him to a pool party at my house that afternoon. He walked up to the house tapping a white cane ("Ooooh"), and brought me a beautiful origami box. The next day I emailed him apologizing for not being helpful about the tomatoes, and offered to bake him a tomato pie as apology (and an excuse to see him again). He wrote back saying he wanted to take me out on his tandem, and to eat my tomato pie (ahem). We married a year and a half later, are about to have a baby, and are packing our house for our own Move by Bike to our first house together.

load amnesia
kirk paulsen

The strangest thing
It's all such a blur, racing to grab items, putting them in my trailer, unloading them at the destination......what did I just haul? I have no idea! I'm just happy to have gone on a bike ride that also just happened to move someone's belongings across town.

Favorite story
I was a part of a group of 30ish people moving someone's stuff, and we were all a giant mass going down a major road. We passed many people with their mouths wide open, but a group of 3 or 4 people that were struggling to lift items into a U-Haul for their own move took a second to catch their breath and asked us what we were doing. The wonderful Steph Routh responded perfectly, saying "We are moving someone's stuff, just like you."

How to Schlep

If moving by bike is unprecedented in your city, town, or community, the first time you move yourself by bike will be everyone else's first, too. It's like stepping on the Moon! You and your intrepid first-time bike movers are explorers. One move with your bike, one giant leap for bike fun! There will be some snags along the way, but you will go into the gilded hero registry of street love as the ones who dared to move by bike. I hope the following tips help glide you past the finish line of the bike move destination.

In spots of the world where bike moving action is already happening, I'd strongly suggest you help out on someone's move before taking the plunge yourself. There are a fair few reasons this makes good horse sense, but topping the charts is building good bike move cred and getting to know those who may just help you move. Other runner-up great reasons include learning how to pack and what to cook (food will feature prominently in this humble little guide, I promise).

Hauling vessels
Some would-be bike movers feel stymied by their perceived lack of bike moving capacity. Fear not! You have greater power than you realize. One of the joys of bike moving is testing the limits of your hauling abilities.

If you have a backpack and no racks, that's just peachy! You can still be a hardcore hauler with just a knapsack. After all, think of the barbells and complete literary works that could fit into the largest backpack you own. Taking small but heavier items in your pack will be useful and much appreciated.

Look at your bicycle as a rack or the beginning of an artistic mobile for a moment. Where could you strap things and still ride? How about a canoe paddle strapped along the top tube, or a few purses dangling from the handlebars? If you have a basket or a front or rear rack, your schleppability factor just rocketed. Panniers or a milk crate strapped to the rear rack helps, too. Think of all the household plants you could move! The bulky toolbox from the garage! A dining room chair!

If you already have a trailer, you will be simply amazed what you can load and lug.

Caution: After a few bike moves, you will feel compelled to build or buy a bigger trailer. This is an avocational hazard; you will not regret succumbing to this compulsion. Remember to pay your rent or mortgage.

blue CAT
by ethan jewett

Before a Dutch mom brought the first Bakfiets to Portland and before Clever Cycles started a family/cargo biking revolution in Portland, Shift, the city's now iconic cycling group, was constantly trying new ideas for having fun with bikes. In May of 2003, Emily Wilson's move from Lloyd district up to the Eliot neighborhood became the perfect excuse to test the concept of a bike move, and it turned out to be a day that would change my thinking about bikes forever.

Back then, there were already a few Xtracycle conversions on the streets, but Robert Burchett was clearly Portland's early adopter when it came to long john-style front load cargo bikes. He owned three at the time, all handmade by Eugene's Center for Appropriate Transport (CAT), and all in service with Magpie Messenger Collective. He was gracious in allowing anyone interested the chance to take a spin . . . I did so the day before Emily's move at the then tiny Mississippi Street Fair. With that vast cargo biking experience under my belt, Robert handed me one of the bikes for the bike move.

When the fifteen bikes and trailers were loaded in front of her house, it was an amazing sight. Her furniture, lamps, clothes, cookware, stereo . . . her life possessions basically, were accounted for on everything from Santana tandems to Blue Sky cargo trailers. My borrowed blue CAT cargo bike was carrying all of Emily's books up front and her box spring and miscellany on a huge CAT trailer Robert had attached. We threaded our way around Lloyd mall and up into North Portland, with a parade atmosphere of music and cheering/honking onlookers now familiar to anyone who's participated in a bike move in the years since.

Needless to say, riding the CAT with a couple hundred pounds of books and a loaded trailer took some getting used to, but the bike clearly wasn't even close to its limits; with mountain bike gearing, I was able to make my way up the short hills to Emily's new digs without any issue.

Shortly after my son was born in 2007, we sold my Honda on Craigslist and bought our first family cargo bike, for a dollar more than the sale price. I've moved on to a much faster (and more CAT-like) Bullitt since then, but seeing what cargo bikes could do firsthand led me to ride one almost exclusively and champion their capabilities for fun, family, and disaster response.

daisy chaining
by amos hunter

First bike move
I found my first bike move on the Shift calendar (I believe it was Fool's move from NW). I was hesitant to show up because I didn't have a trailer, but the description said racks and bags would be helpful too, so I gave it a go. I was pleasantly surprised that even my small capacity was useful, and I met some great new future friends!

Toughest load
I think the biggest load I ever had was a double trailer setup, consisting of a burley and an Adam George flatbed, daisy-chained together. It was actually pretty easy to haul, but making wide turns in the thick of the group called for some creative traffic direction.

The strangest thing
I once hauled a household full of potted plants via flatbed. I looked like a rolling atrium.

Favorite story
One time coming off the Broadway Bridge someone in the group made a sudden stop, and those of us coming down the ramp had to do the same behind him. Your beloved zine author stopped her bike in time, but her body followed Newton's law. Fortunately she managed to do the most amazing ninja tuck-and-roll down the sidewalk, all the while protecting the expensive electronics she was carrying. The maneuver ended in a perfect 10.0 stuck landing on her feet, and the smile never left her face.

What to bring

Make sure your bike and trailer are in good repair. Tune it up and pump up the tires. Blowing a tire or killing a brake cable is Not Fun during a bike move (particularly on a downhill). You might be riding a lot, so double-check that your water bottle and tools are also on board.

Bring whatever hauling vessels you have that you feel comfortable using. If the trailer is new to you, ride it around unloaded to get a feel for the handling (and dimensions).

Used bike innertubes, panniers, backpacks, cargo nets bungee cords, packing straps, duct tape, string, tarp, and small padding equipment are all neat ideas to have with you. At the very least, bring some used innertubes. You will need them! Even if the move organizer has some innertubes, you can bet he/she won't have enough for everyone.

beware the broken weld
by josh guttmacher

Why I joined my first bike move
Peer pressure.

Toughest load
I felt like I had a hernia for a long time after the Rebuilding Center Deconstruction move because I used a barely functioning kid's trailer with a broken weld that led me to get off my bike and drag it through every turn. I bought a much better trailer for $40 and am psyched to move more heavy lumber!

The strangest thing
A 680 pound beam.

bathtub brigade
steve couche

Toughest Load
I hauled a steel bathtub with someone in it...the person had to get out on some of the (even) gentle hills, but we made it to the bathtub museum's new digs.

Favorite Story
Moved someone's office/art materials/supplies to her SE Bybee new location on a damp day, and was totally impressed with her daughter's (10 yrs old I believe) trailer haul the full distance.

I'd also like to thank Mr. Bamboo trailer (Adam) for designing and building such an awesome trailer! It is a joy to haul with.

What to wear

You're going to be hauling, maybe for miles. Bring comfy clothing that you can get warm and sweaty in. If it's a costume ride, do it up! Remember you still need to ride safely, so tutus before togas. The weather could also do some crazy things. This could mean bringing anything from rain pants to sunscreen to snow tires. Check the weather forecast before you head out, but don't hitch your star to a favorable prediction.

the mustache ride?

by erinne goodell

First bike move

I don't remember the first move I helped with, but the first one I went to was really unorganized - he hadn't even packed a lot of his stuff. I ended up leaving that time before loading. But I have helped with a couple dozen moves by now. My impression has always been one of amazement that a group of friends and complete strangers are willing to give up a chunk of their weekend (they're 90% on the weekends) to move someone's stuff. Because they can. And because it is a chance to get together with friends and make new ones.

Bike move confession

I felt bad making people move my rock collection in each of my three bike moves, so I hid lots of bags of rocks in other things.

Favorite story

I have really loved some of the theme moves, like Magnum PI vs Lumberjacks. Marina knit a whole bunch of mustaches for those of us who can't grow our own, and as we rode along we had one woman yell out (innocently, I think), "Hey! Is that a mustache ride?"

Pack it, strap it

Loading up is probably my favorite part of a bike move. If you love playing Tetris or spatial puzzles, you will love the load-up process. Gah! I love it so much.

If it's your first time helping with a bike move, you might start with medium-weight boxes. Add a houseplant for flair! Once you're feeling comfortable with, say, a child's trailer (this might take a few moves), level up with a little verticality or bulk: an upside-down easy chair on top of boxes, a floor lamp, or an ironing board.

While you're strapping things down, try to eyeball which items might be most precariously placed. Either strap those down better or kick them to the curb for someone else to haul. Be mindful that nothing rubs against your trailer tires or inhibits your ability to pedal, steer, or see. Once you've strapped everything down, give it a good hearty jostle. If anything's feeling slippery, adjust the tie-downs or lose some of your load (better to lose it now than along the ride!). Is any of the trailer load rubbing or threatening to rub against your rear bicycle tire? Is the trailer bottoming out in the middle? Repack it all. A solidly tied down load should feel like one big mass when you shove it around; a shove should rock the trailer tires.

Once you're loaded up and tied down, take it for a test spin down the block. Try to make a U-turn. If anything's rubbing against the tires or feeling slippery or top-heavy, adjust the packing until the issue abates.

Do all that and boom! You're ready to roll with your parade float!

One thing I learned on my 58th bike move: when in doubt, check the load weight. I loaded up what I thought were individually lighter items (headboard, end tables, easy chair, etc). I could turn and brake, but the uphills were tough! Imagine my embarrassment when the hitch snapped 1/2 mile in, and I realized I had loaded probably upwards of 600 lbs. Ooops!

PRO TIPS: PACKING
- Pilates ball? Cargo net. Trust me
- Find one moving item that makes you giggle and display it prominently on your load
- Dear men, please do not stand around a female mover and suggest how she should load her trailer, unless she asks your advice. Resist the urge to "mansplain"
- Wrestling with taut rubber at the end of a load can be damning. If you're strapping down with used innertubes, experiment with ways to both snugly tie and then easily un-tie. You could also bring a pocket knife to cut the tubes during the unloading process, but you'll waste part of the tubes for next time.
- Hauling someone's little pet in a kennel or aquarium? Pack with plenty of cushion underneath and shade/cover above. Ideally, have the pet where you can see it (like a front rack). Pack very, very, very humanely!
- Remember that it's not just about how much you can haul, but how well you can brake. Ask yourself: could you stop on a downhill with that load?

trailer virgin
by maria schur

Toughest load
The most difficult thing was keeping track of my new width while dragging a small trailer. I was a trailer virgin and ran over a median at one point. Just like all other things bike, you bite off little bits at a time, block by block, and it all works out.

The strangest thing
I was delighted to be given a trailer full of bicycle tires because I work at a bike shop that specializes in tires, and I consider myself a tire nut!

of geriatric rats and young children
by katie proctor

First bike move

My first bike move was April Wiza's. The starting point for her move was not far from my house, so I ventured out with my husband and our five-month-old baby, Jasper. As my cargo boxes were already half-full of baby, we snuggled some other fragile things into the other half: some houseplants, some glass bottles, and April's geriatric pet rat. As she placed the cage in my bike, I remember her saying, "This rat is very old. If she dies before we get there, it's probably not your fault." Very reassuring. (The rat was fine.)

Favorite story

Kristi Falkowski moved on a very cold day. I had my son, Jasper, then about 2.5, along for the ride in his behind-the-handlebars front seat. The temperature continued to drop as we rode, and it was eventually near freezing. Jasper's hands and feet were getting very cold in spite of his warm gloves and socks, and he went from fussing to crying as we got stuck at a long light. Then, Lauren Pedersen passed by us with her big white fluffy cat-eared helmet, and Jasper perked up. "She has kitty ears!" "She does! What color are they?" Typical toddler engagement talk. "They are white. Mama, what color are MY kitty ears?" "Ummm... what color do you want your kitty ears to be?" "Mine are pink! And big! Yours are black! And floppy!" He was completely distracted, and proceeded to describe what kind of (imaginary) animal ears everyone around us was wearing. Folks began to play along, and we made it to the end of the ride with no more tears.

I know that not a lot of the bike move community has kids, and that a freaked-out kid can bring down the mood of an otherwise upbeat space. Having so many people willing to engage and cheer up my kiddo was a truly wonderful thing.

Road Etiquette

You are now loaded up and on your way down the road as part of a crazy stuff parade. The experience of hauling a bunch of goods in a group is a unique and heady feeling. While you might be inclined to ride like you're in a parade, remember that rules of the road still apply.

Communication with other crew members and road users is key. If there's glass, a pothole or a bollard to be avoided, call it out ("Glass!" "Hole!" "Post!") and point to it. Also call out when you're slowing down or stopping ("Slowing!" "Stopping!"). Call out cars in front ("Car up!"), behind ("Car back!"), or to either side through an intersection. Repeat calls that you hear so that others know what's happening.

The move organizer, corkers, and sweep are the bosses. Listen to them and do as they say. If you hear "Car up!" or "Car back," try to get into a single file line – or as close as you can safely – to allow them to get past. The sooner a car passes the group, the less you all have to worry about them. If you are near the front of the line and you choose not to move over for a car, that means everyone behind you has to deal with riding near that car (and likely an increasingly pissed driver) until you choose to grace the right side of the road with your presence.

Be gracious to others on the road. They didn't plan for this bike move, and their thoughts might be on other concerns. Most people will be thrilled to see you and will want to take pictures and wave. That's the fun! It gets even better if you remember to wave and thank them for waiting and for supporting you. The more you can make everyone feel proud to be some part of a bike move – as a schlepper, passerby, or driver waiting for you to clear the intersection – the easier and more fun the next bike move will be. If you encounter someone driving aggressively and generally being a jackass, try to stay calm (I know it's tough!) and focus on keeping everyone safe. If a little smug pity helps you get through the moment, tell yourself they're just sad and jealous because they didn't join the bike move.

PRO TIPS: ROAD ETIQUETTE
- Always wave at and ring your bell for small children!
- To the extent possible, ride in a straight line. This will steady your load and help others bike near you
- If the ride gets separated by a red light or a mechanical malfunction, call it up the line
- When in doubt, take a deep breathe and be nice

"hey man, you gotta calm down"
by kristin bott

The strangest thing

I've ridden other people's bikes. I've moved the wedding dress of a bride-to-be. I've jumped off of my bike to push a loaded Aaron Tarfman up a hill. I think the strangest things are the combination of normal things – the piles of shoes and dishes and books and random crap. You get to see what people's weak "stuff" spots are – they collect pens or old china or have 10,000 scraps of paper for a project. It's the perfect midpoint of support and snooping, really – you have a glimpse into people's lives, but then you avert your eyes because you have to watch where you're riding.

Favorite story

Riding down Tillamook St., at the back of the pack with Steph, there was a car behind us driven by a person who was Having Very Strong Feelings. Specifically, they were being aggressive and violent with their car, lots of revving and honking and general harrassment. Steph and I held our place in the road while waving and/or shaking our fingers (depending on the stage of the escalation)...

...and there was some punk-ass high school kid on a skateboard, his friend on a BMX bike. They were going about our pace, and then the guy on the skateboard pulled out his smartphone and started recording the entire thing. I remember him (or his friend) saying things like HEY MAN, YOU GOTTA CALM DOWN and HEY, THAT'S NOT COOL. It felt great to have random people have our (literal, proverbial) back.

Also, I've met some of my closest friends on bike moves.

bike temple
by scott lieuallen

Toughest load
I pulled an electric organ when we moved the Bike Temple. It weighed
at least a couple hundred pounds. We put in on large cargo trailer.
How did I do it? Slowly.

Favorite story
My best story was when we were moving Ben Foote out of Old Town.
I was riding next to O'Leary when someone I didn't know asked how
long the move was. We looked at each other and shrugged. I said,
"We don't know. We drink coffee, we load up, we ride and yak with
everybody for awhile then we drink beer and party some more."
The whole thing is a party.

deconstruction bike moves
by ted buehler

Household bike moves are fun and all, but there's usually not
enough heavy furniture to go around to satisfy folks with a
serious freight-hauling fetish.

I've bought a lot of lumber and other heavy stuff at "The Rebuilding
Center", a local salvage warehouse in Portland, OR. They're a
nonprofit that deconstructs houses and sells the material. They
had the idea they could get bike volunteers to help haul an entire
house, and invited me to coordinate a "Deconstruction Bike Move".

Over two weekends, we had 35 volunteers come and haul four flatbed
truck loads of lumber from a deconstruction site to the warehouse.
In total, we moved about 18,000 lbs of material total in about
100 trips. We all had a blast. Everyone got to pull multiple long,
heavy bulky loads. We made a little scene as we paraded across the
neighborhood, and we did the work of 16 miles of truck-driving.

Here's some tips on hauling lumber:
- Load your trailer so the center of gravity is just forward of the axle.
- Tie stuff down with inner tubes, watch out for nails.
- For long loads, use two trailers. Attach a milk crate securely to the front trailer, then loosely tie the load to the milk crate so it can twist a bit and pivot up to 180 degrees. Tie the load securely to the back trailer.
- Drink lots of water.

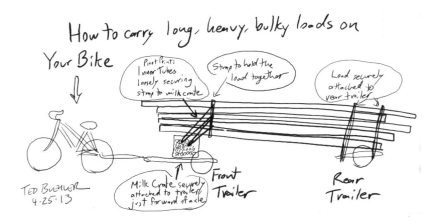

How to carry long, heavy, bulky loads on Your Bike

Pivot Point: Inner Tubes loosely securing strap to milk crate

Strap to hold the load together

Load securely attached to rear trailer

Milk Crate securely attached to trailer just forward of axle

Front Trailer

Rear Trailer

TED BUEHLER
4-25-13

how to

ORGANIZE

a

bike

move

Organizing a bike move is like preparing to move to a new house and planning a crazy birthday party at the same time. You'll love doing it, but at some point in the organizing process, you might just wonder whether all the planning will be worth it in the end.

It will. It will be epicly worthy it.

Don't Fret ... Too Much
I organized my first bike move one chilly January day in 2007. I had already helped with a half dozen bike moves, so I had some small idea of what I was signing up for. However, I'm a natural worrier, and boy did I worry about the bike move! Even though I had downsized my stuff, and even though I had created and widely spread invitations to the bike move, I fretted that there would be too much for folks to move and not enough people to move it. Though I had mapped and ridden the route a number of times (as well as possible alternate routes), I was nail-bitingly concerned that the hills would be too steep, the street traffic too great, the intersections too dangerous.

The big day came, and 22 people – a few of whom I had never met! - showed up. There was no problem moving all of my stuff; in fact, a few intrepids were seen good-naturedly quibbling over who would get to move the crazier items (like my stage-fighting sword collection). The route was fine, and people appreciated the work put into it. We moved all of my worldly possessions gently uphill seven miles within three hours, including loading and unloading time. My Mom was there to greet us at the new house with lasagna, hot soup, a stoked fire, and plenty of beer. We ended with a four-hour gala housewarming party. In the end, I was glad I planned a lot and fretted a little before bike move day.

If you are contemplating a bike move to your next abode, do it! Unleash your inner planner, bite your nails, gather your troops, brew your cauldrons, and then enjoy the ride. Not a natural-born planner but know someone who is? Enlist her/him!

The following steps and tips might make organizing a bike move seem a bit more daunting than it actually is. Take what you think is useful and leave the rest (except the part about the beer and food).

trailers on loan
by noel mickelberry

First bike move

My first bike move was my own move. I had heard stories of bike moves but had never even thought it possible until I realized how many people own trailers, and how much junk those trailers can hold!

I was nervous for my move - what if people didn't show up? What if we couldn't carry all of my stuff? I had collected about 7 extra trailers, as I knew a lot of people who wanted to help but didn't have trailers, and people with trailers who couldn't make it that day. I even had a trike with hauling capacity ready if someone wanted to ride it (no one did).

I borrowed a giant trailer and jam-packed it with as much stuff as possible before anyone arrived, because I wanted to make sure people didn't feel overwhelmed. All of a sudden, people started showing up - even people I didn't know! Soon I was frantically unpacking my trailer and racing around the house to find things that I didn't think we'd have room for - my snowboard! My tent! The last muffins from breakfast! It was outstanding.

Favorite story

When the yard, driveway, sidewalk and street were overflowing with people - that was pretty incredible. When you couldn't even see the entire bike move while riding through neighborhoods. People with boom boxes on their bikes playing music and just enjoying the ride. That was all awesome!

a straddling queen
brian scrivener

First move
My first was Emily Wilson's bike move in May 2003, the first ever
organized using Shift and the earliest bike move in Portland that
I'm aware of. When she suggested it, I thought it was the greatest
idea in less-consumption that I'd ever heard of: a magical combination
of pollution-reduction, collaborative effort, and food.

Toughest load
With a large cargo trailer, nothing seems difficult. Refrigerator,
clothes dryer, whatever ... just set it down and strap it on. I did
once move a queen mattress using a child trailer: it straddled my
bike's luggage rack (with two bike buckets giving more stability)
and the top bar of the trailer.

1. Choosing a date and time

Choose a weekend day and invite your friends, family, and anyone you know who has a bike and a sense of adventure.

If your moving date is dictated by that little sliver of time between the end of one lease and the beginning of another, well, that's the date you've got. Love the date you're with! If you have a little flexibility, though, you might check to see that there are no other competing major bike events, weddings, or festivals that could whittle away your potential bike move crew.

A late morning start time generally seems to work well: this gives people time to make their way to your house comfortably, and it still gives the sense that there's plenty of time to get everything accomplished.

> **PRO TIPS: DATE AND TIME**
> • As a general rule, assume bike movers will ride at about 4-5 miles an hour (less if there's significant elevation gain or a lot of busy intersections). Plan a start time that gets everyone there with plenty of daylight left
> • If there's a raucous event planned the night before your move date, consider pushing the start time back to a little later in the day
> • Daylight Savings days are confusing, and there are statistically more traffic crashes around these days

2. Finding a route

Most of the bike moving experience will be spent actually riding. Here's where you get to plan a parade that gets everyone there safely!

First and foremost, you owe your bike moving crew a safe ride. Nothing else trumps this. You are responsible for the safeguarding of your team from car traffic, seat-cracking pavement, and extreme gravity to the best of your mortal abilities.

If your city has a bike map, use that as a starting point to plot your bike move adventure. That map should show which streets are busy and which intersections are gnarly. A bike map is a great starting point, but the next part is where the magic happens. I find that routing through calm residential streets is generally better than using bike lanes on busier streets, and those residential streets might not be highlighted on the bike map. Have some fun checking out possible paths through neighborhoods. You are an artist, and the map is your canvas! Find a calm route with as few turns, hills and traffic stops as possible, and you will have a solid work of art. Ensure smooth pavement, and your route will be a masterpiece! As a bonus for doing this work, you get to know your new neighborhood.

Sometimes there is just no avoiding a memorable hill or a few busy intersections. Let folks know about any riding challenges before the move and also while people are loading up. This helps parents decide whether and how their children can participate; it also helps people decide how heavily they should load their trailers.

Got a route? Awesome! Now ride it a couple of times. Which are the busy intersections? How will you get everyone through safely (please see "To Cork or Not to Cork?")? Are there any gravelly or heavily pot-holed roads? If so, try to find a more amenable road. Get a feel for where your turns are so you can lead the ride with confidence.

Pro Tips: route
- Check out any city- or county-wide events (parades, presidential visits, etc) that might impact traffic on your route
- Brunch locations and parks are incredibly cool to ride past. Maximize your parade route fun!
- Left turns on busy streets suck. Even if it takes three rights to make your left, they're probably worth it
- Look out for pinch points. Bollards on multi-use paths and diverters meant to keep cars out can also confound the trailer hauling your mattress. Matt Picio uses a measuring tape at potential pinch points
- Around is better than over. The truly nerdy refer to a topographical map (your cartographilic friends are standing by to assist you!)

extreme bike moving

by matt picio

Ok, so you've done a bike move. Now you're looking for that extra challenge (or perhaps you just have something really heavy, or live far out there). It's time for an Extreme Bike Move™.

Moving long-distance

Moving long distances requires a little extra planning. First off, be up-front with everyone. You can still get people out to a 12-mile bike move, just advertise it as an epic or extreme move, and you'll get the "hard core" element. It's better to be honest about the distance (and perhaps pad it out a little to the next 1/2 mile mark) rather than telling people "it's just a bit over 8 miles" when it's really twelve. Make sure the start point has water available and a bathroom, and remind people 10 minutes before the start of both items.

A long distance means you should have food at both the start and the end for your bike movers. Plan the route along the flattest route possible, and if you have to have an uphill climb and have a choice when it occurs, try to plan for it to happen as late in the ride as possible. Most importantly, the move leader (hopefully that's you!) should keep a deliberately slower-than-normal pace, especially if anyone in the move is more heavily loaded. What feels slow at the start will be a lot more challenging once you're 8+ miles into the ride.

Long rides means it's a lot more likely you'll be crossing busy roads, so ensure that everyone knows whether the ride is being corked, and how that's being handled. If you have time and skills to make a map, do so - and ensure that all the movers have your cell phone number - longer rides increase the chance of someone getting lost or making a wrong turn along the way, especially if it's a larger move. The conditions that tend to aggravate riders (loud noises, heavy/fast traffic, bumpy roads) get much more annoying further into the longer rides, so the longer the ride, the more you'll need to minimize the factors which make it unpleasant.

Moving heaven and earth (heavy items)

Moving heavy items by bike can be especially challenging. Couches, beds, desks, refrigerators, stoves, and pianos have all been moved on Portland bike moves - even a loaded gun cabinet! (the cabinet was loaded, not the guns) In addition to having more than one person to move them, and watching out for corners, you also have to be careful not to overload the trailer, and to load it properly.

When loading a heavy item onto a bike trailer, you'll want the weight as low as possible, and centered over the axle. Too much weight forward will put stress on the hitch, and may cause it to break. Too much weight in back will drastically affect the handling of both trailer and bike, and can even cause a crash. All commercial trailers will have a rated weight - be aware of that weight and be very careful if you think the item might exceed it. Heavy items are less prone to shift, but when they do, it's much more serious - so try to secure the item extra well with additional bungees, rope, tubes, or whatever - if you can but it up against part of the trailer frame to secure it, so much the better, but try to keep it centered left to right and over the axle. Particularly long items can be laid across the trailer at an angle, but try to keep them as balanced as possible, and keep a close eye when turning. Also keep an eye how far to the side the item sticks out to ensure you don't hit parked cars or other obstacles.

As with long bike moves, if anyone is hauling extra-heavy loads, you should try to minimize hills, keep an easy pace, and check in periodically to ensure that the pace is OK.

To Cork or Not to Cork?

Cork = v. To utilize one's body and bicycle to stop oncoming traffic for the purpose of allowing a group of cyclists to pass through the intersection without stopping.

The practice of corking is a time-honored tradition of bike fun that allows a covey of riders to stick together in one cohesive group. During bike moves, corking provides another essential function: it allows schleppers of larger, heavier loads to keep their momentum rather than having to stop and painstakingly start back up frequently.

Corking is not strictly legal, as you can imagine. While police officers and road construction flaggers have been imbued with legal authority to stop traffic, corkers have not. It can be argued that, done correctly, corking is a safety measure during bike moves and incurs little enough traffic interruption that the practice is benign. Don't expect police officers to come to that view, though! Veteran movers differ on the practice of corking; I believe in highlighting the fun and minimizing the potential road drama. For intersections with stop signs and/or light oncoming traffic, corking is relatively low-stress and generally appreciated. Given the number of drivers who stop for bike moves on lower traffic streets anyway, I'd argue corking provides good, clean communication between people driving and bike moving.

Corking busy streets is a lot rougher on everyone. The few times I've corked a busy intersection, I've felt anywhere between embarrassed and apologetic to physically threatened. It's really not fun to cork urban highways. If you are planning the route, please try to reduce as many unprotected busy crossings as possible. Routing through signalized intersections (crossings with traffic lights) is the easiest way to avoid corking busy streets. You can also make very clear at the beginning of the ride that you will wait for those who didn't make it through the intersection. If there are a number of traffic signals in a row before turning, get through all of them separately and then wait on the other side for everyone to meet back up.

A good corker is a friendly ambassador of bike fun. They go out into the intersection with loaded bike and wave at drivers. They smile. Often times, folks will roll down their windows and ask what's going on. The friendly corker tells onlookers about the bike move until the crew is almost through the intersection. I like to give a 5-second countdown with my hands and then finish with a huge wave and a smile before leaving the intersection. If people are upset, apologize and say that the ride is only doing this at a very few intersections, then thank them for their patience.

I said corking is unlawful. There is, actually, a more legal alternative. In Oregon (and most other states, I believe), every corner is a legal crosswalk – marked or unmarked. Pedestrians have right of way, as long as they have dipped a toe or bicycle wheel into the roadway and have given oncoming traffic ample time to stop. A lightly-loaded corker or two can dismount to the crosswalk and walk alongside the other bike movers streaming by, proceeding in the crosswalk until everyone is through.

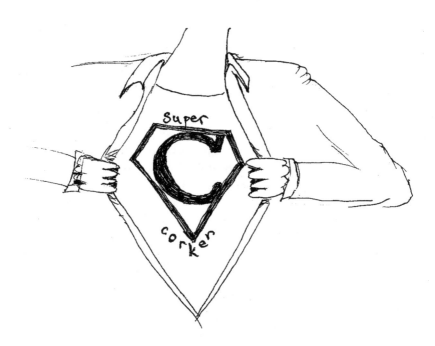

3. Getting the word out

You have a date and time. You have a start and end point.
It's time to tell the world about your upcoming stuff parade!

Portland, Oregon has a group called Shift that connects via an
online listserve and calendar for fun bike events like bike moves
(www.shift2bikes.org). If yours is a Portland-area bike move,
post your move both on the listserve and the calendar.

What to include in your posts:
- Date / Time - include gather time and load-up time
(eg. 10:00am gather and drink coffee, 10:30am load up)
- Start Location – address
- End Location – neighborhood (you don't need to give a
specific address, but it's good to let people know generally
where the ride is ending so they can plan how to get home)
- Biking Distance – include number of miles and if the
route is generally flat, uphill, or downhill. Is the route
child-friendly?
- What to Wear – rain pants and/or costumes?
- Food & Beverage – boast your pre- and post-move menu to
entice people to come!
- RSVP / Contact info.

Wherever you live, try to post your bike move where people who
love to bike will see it. Some ways to get the word out: Facebook
event and posts, Twitter, email invitations, written invitations
(these can also make great souvenirs!), and/or ¼ page flyers
to pass out to friends, etc.

Bike moves can be great stories for the media. If you have
organized a bike move before and know you'll have bandwidth
and a healthy attendance on the big day, you might consider
letting local press know. Print and radio media are generally
lower stress to deal with than television cameras during the bike
move, as a point of information. If your bike move is a first for
you, though, you'll probably want to hold off on contacting
media beforehand. Either way, you could spread the word to
media after the fact (please see "Giving Back" below).

Pro Tips: tell the world
- Have at least one type of invitation to which people can RSVP. This will help you plan for food and contingencies
- Send invitations as soon as you know the bike move will happen, and then send reminders one week and one day out
- Highlight just how astonishingly fun this bike move is going to be (because it will be)

pedal power
audrey addison

Toughest load

My most memorable, after my own, had to be Steph and Ed's bike move, with 70 folks helping out and "schlepping" out. It never fails to amaze me that strangers who don't even know the person moving will show up to help with a bike move, just for the fun of it! It is a great way to socialize and show off trailers and how awkward and heavy objects are no match for pedaling power. And they go quicker and are so much more enjoyable than the "two guys and a truck version"!

bikeasaurus
by becky morton

Toughest load

Huge, amazingly heavy counter for my business. I assumed I would have to come back later and move it with a truck. But someone showed up with a large bamboo trailer connected to two bikes. There was no hesitation. People just loaded it up, and the counter was moved by bike!

Favorite story

Moving my business (BIKEASAURUS) by bike is one of my favorite memories. Forty-three people showed up. There wasn't even enough stuff to fill all the trailers. I think a couple of people ended up carrying trailers full of empty trailers. There were things I assumed would be too heavy to move, but I was wrong. Everything in the store was moved by bike. It was, without a doubt, the most efficient and fun way I could have possibly moved my business.

4. Packing it up

Your friends and fellow bike funnists have signed up to help you move by bike, not to pack your flotsam. When asked their biggest pet peeve, veteran bike movers replied that their #1 hair-puller is showing up to a bike move when nothing's packed. It should go without saying: pack before your move.

Downsize! There has never been a better time to slough off some of your unneeded possessions than before a bike move. Consider a naked lady party before your move; this is not only a great way to winnow your wardrobe, but it's also one more way to get the word out about your impending event.

Pack your things beforehand with some thought to distributing weight. Small boxes and bags are highly recommended. If you have a barbell collection, for example, you might consider splitting up the weights into your clothing and bedding boxes.

PRO TIPS: PACKING UP
• Use colored dots or a permanent marker to identify which boxes go into which room at your home-to-be
• Plan to move the fragile and most sentimental/valuable things yourself. Is there anything that would devastate you if it were broken en route? Yeah, put that aside, because it's going with you
• If you are living with roommates who are staying at your soon-to-be-former residence, make sure it is clear which stuff is going and which isn't
• Leave the broom/vacuum at the old house so you can do a final clean-up after the move.

caution: sentimental value
by babs adamski

First bike move
Ayleen put out the call when she bought her house. . . I think that was my first move. Very sweet, very fun. And she had a boat that some badass guy hauled. I remember being amazed and feeling edgy about stopping car traffic. Most people were cool.

Many bike moves later, I was glad to do it myself when I moved from Alberta to St. Johns.

Toughest load
A chest of drawers that was given to me when I was in high school. It was small and not really that difficult to pack but just precious to me and I wanted it to make it to my new home unscarred.

the list of strange
halley weaver

The strangest thing
I have a broad definition of strange. I've hauled a bathtub museum! clawfoot tubs, cats - I move a harp regularly - mattresses, a russian porcelain tea set (that was probably the scariest) - a trumpet player, a ukelele player, a photographer (while taking photos), mannequins, recycling bins, bamboo, old xmas trees, groceries, several bikes (including a bikes/sidecar and tallbike all at once).

Favorite story
I was sick with the flu in wintertime and a friend was having a bike move on a Thursday or Friday night. Only about 6 people showed up for her bike move. She was tweeting that she needed help so I got bundled up, hitched up and showed up. I showed up as everyone was arriving back for round two. I was just the trailer amount they needed. And I scored a Chrome backpack from her freebox! When we got to the destination, they unloaded my trailer first so I could get back home to bed. Helped a friend out, got a backpack, all for an hour of fresh air and compromising my flu.

5. Food

Next to planning the route, food is the most important aspect of a successful bike move. Food is so important to the success of bike moves that we gave the issue its own section later in this zine, complete with rockstar recipes!

Prepping food for a bunch of people in the midst of all these other tasks can seem daunting. Do you have a friend or family member who likes cooking? Ask them to help you, particularly if you think there will be a bundle of people. Being a part of a bike move is incredibly fun, but not everyone wants to (or can) bike. Inviting non-biking, kitchen-savvy friends or family members to help prepare food is a way to involve them in an epic event.

You won't know precisely how many people are coming. It's a nail-biting truth of bike moves. Prepare food for the upper limit of your predicted attendance. For Ed and my bike move in January 2013, I thought 45-50 people might come. On the day of, we counted 70 people in attendance. Luckily, we had plenty of food help from members of our family, a few friends, and our real estate agent and home loan broker (thanks, guys)!

Food and beverage will be your biggest cost of the bike move. Be comfortable with that. Remember that you are planning not just a move, but also a housewarming party and an event that you will all remember for a long time.

At the start location, have coffee and breakfast munchies in hearty quantities. Coffee, tea, juice, bananas, donuts, and bagels are good low-key, pre-move food options.

The end location is also the party location. Many veteran bike movers love pizza as a post-move food, and that is certainly easier on the food prep tip than homemade deliciousness. Pizza is easier, but it can also be more expensive and less friendly to some dietary restrictions. Do what feels best for you.

Booze and beverages are critical for post-move merriment.

In the Portland area, beer has become an expectation at the end of a stuff parade. It doesn't have to be the finest beer, but it does have to be plentiful. Ed and I had a chilled keg from Upright Brewing waiting at the finish line of our 70-person bike move. I believe that is a major reason why our move is well remembered! We also had wine, gluten-free beer, and plenty of juice to try to make everyone feel appreciated.

Pro Tips: food

• Look at your RSVP list and consider dietary needs. Check out recipes in this book for ideas on gluten-free and vegan comestibles. Same thing goes for beverages.

• Having leftovers is a much better option than running out of food

• If you are ordering pizza for your post-move food, try to get the food there as soon after the moving crew arrives as possible. This might mean calling with a specific pick-up time, or entrusting pick-up to a reliable friend.

• Seriously, do not forget the beer!

taco bar
by chris mccraw

My own bike move was a little ridiculous. The first two guys who showed up got pretty close to fisticuffs about who got to tow my fridge across town.

Since I can't feed people crappy food, we had a breakfast-taco bar while folks loaded up. Even before the last bite was eaten, someone was packing up the dishes and fridge contents onto their cargo bike and we were getting ready to roll. Downstairs, my driveway and my neighbor's driveway are full of 40-odd cyclists, whose bikes are full of a lifetime of stuff, a cat in a box, and a keg mounted for rolling access on Ed's cargo cruiser. We rolled downhill for one mile and uphill for three. At the end of the ride, there was beer, there was pizza, and there was naked trampolining. My neighbors came to join the party, since it was hard to ignore, and there was much rejoicing.

I can certainly wait to move again, but fortunately i don't have to wait to bike move again, since bike moves happen more than once a month (sometimes more than one the same day!) here.

Don't Be That Guy

People love a well-organized bike move. I know I do. The world is an unpredictable place, and of course there will always be that special something that surprises you on bike move day. That said, there are plenty of wrinkles you can avoid with some thought. Veteran bike movers shared their biggest pet peeves here.

Don't be that guy who . . .
  ... fails to pack for the move (this was #1 on the peeve list!)
  ... wakes up late for his/her own bike move
  ... has friends "help" with their trucks during the procession
  ... corks aggressively busy streets
  ... rides unpredictably during the haul
  ... makes a top-heavy load that will inevitably flip during the ride
  ... complains
  ... heckles drivers
  ... crams fun stuff (documentary making, etc) at the beginning of the bike move (when people just want to load and go)

6. Contingencies

Part of the fascination of moving by bike is the element of surprise. You think 30 people will come, and either 45 or 11 show up instead. The weather forecast in May calls for sunshine, but there is a snow flurry during your bike move. You haven't invited any media, but behold! There is a news reporter from your city's daily fish wrapper with their memo pad in hand. Surprise!

Too many/few bike movers – Usually, bike moves magically have a perfect number of movers come. While this is generally true, it is not universally true, so planning ahead for possible snags is a swell idea. Just in case too few people show up or there is too little carrying capacity for your moving needs, you might want to set the start time to allow for a second load. Alternately, you might want to have a friend's truck secured as back-up (there, I said it. You might possibly still need a motorized contraption for clean-up). If you are moving a short distance – say, less than three miles – you could probably just do a second bike move. For 6+ mile bike moves, however, that's not going to happen. Ask a friend to use her/his truck as back-up and hope you don't have to use it. If too many bike movers show up, add water to the soup and ask people not to be greedy with their loads.

Weather – It happens. In Portland, that usually means rain. Tarps and garbage bags work really well. Remind people to bring their rain clothes. If it's summer or unseasonably hot, remind people to bring water bottles, and put sunscreen next to the pre-move donuts. For bonus points, douse people with the garden hose before heading out.

Media - You might think I'm joking about the media unexpectedly coming to your move. As I was welcoming folks to my first bike move in 2007, I found myself greeting a documentary crew. They came with movie cameras and waivers on clipboards and asked if they could film the move. It ended up being awesome! One of the cameramen rode in someone's trailer the entire way. Hilarious! If you feel overwhelmed and want someone from the media to get out of your space, though, introduce them to someone whom you know is good at talking (even better if they're a veteran mover), and then focus on other things.

PRO TIPS: CONTINGENCIES
- If it's two days in advance of the move day and you honestly think you're not going to get enough bike movers, do not be afraid to sound desperate. Threaten the use of a truck (the horror!)
- Check out the nearest grocery or convenience story to your home-to-be in case you need to make a beer or food run
- Make sure your cell phone's charged for the day of
- First aid kits rock.

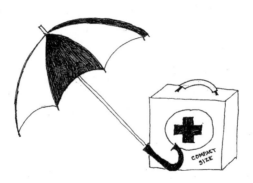

the fish survived
by beth hamon

I created my OWN bike move in 1997. I was ready to live in shared housing with people who actually engaged in conversation now and then. Found an ideal situation but I did not own a car. I organized a few friends, and we took seven or eight trips with three bike trailers, back and forth between NW Industrial (long before anyone called "The Pearl") and Humboldt neighborhood (North Portland). It took all day.

The strangest thing
A friend's aquarium. Half-filled with water and fish, covered with layers of tin foil secured with duct tape. Lashed to one side of my Surly Big Dummy on the wide-loader "shelf". I rode slowly and carefully, and the fish survived.

7. The Day Of

Your work is pretty well done by this point. Congratulations!
Deep breathe.

Here's a checklist of things to remember on Bike Move Day.

Before the move
- Set your alarm and be sure to wake up before your bike move.
I shouldn't have to say this, but …
- Charge your phone
- If possible, make some copies of your route for the "corkers"
and "sweep" to use
- Do a once-over of your goods to make sure you haven't
forgotten to pack anything
- Brew your coffee and prep your pre-move food
- If you have anyone helping with post-move food and beverage,
check in with them and make sure they have the house key
- If your floor needs to be covered (for carpet or cleat reasons),
do that

When people arrive
- Greet everyone and tell them where the food is
- If some stuff is staying behind, announce to everyone what
is going and what is not
- Load up your trailer, but only lightly (you will be leading
this ride and need to be nimble)
- If some intersections need to be "corked," enlist corkers
(see "To Cork or Not to Cork"). Ideally, these people do not
have trailers or have light loads
- Find someone to "sweep" – a person who rides at the back
of the move and makes sure no one is left behind. Have a
copy of the route to give him/her
- Before the ride starts, gather everyone together. Thank
everyone for coming, announce the general route and key
challenging intersections, define riding rules and etiquette,
identify sweep to the group, and then invite everyone to
saddle up and ride behind you

Enjoy the ride!

At the destination
- Unlock the doors and make sure food and beverages are either ready to go or on their way
- Tell folks which room is which for unpacking
- Thank everyone again
- Let the housewarming party begin!

PRO TIPS
- Make signs for the bathroom in each location and the name of each room in the new place, if it's not clear
- When you identify the challenging intersections to the group, be very clear about what will happen at those intersections
- Have a circulation plan for unloading (eg in through the back door and out through the front door)
- Let your new and future neighbors know that you're planning a bike move and what they can expect.
- Chill out on move day. Seriously. If it hasn't been done by the day of the move, it's probably out of your control. Roll with the punches and enjoy the ride.

8. Giving Back

Your bike move is done, and your worldly possessions are now installed in your new house. Get a good night's sleep. When you wake up, realize what just happened: a bundle of people just took time out of their day to help you do something important to you. Now is the time to be grateful and to give back.

Send an email, Twitter, and/or Facebook post thanking everyone who came. Lavish praise. If someone took pictures of the ride, make sure to link to those photos (with permission) in as many places as you can. Give a special shout out to anyone who helped you behind the scenes: with food, planning, corkers and sweep, route planning, or day-of heroes. Your bike movers just did something very cool for you. Tell them all about it, and give them an opportunity to respond with their favorite stories from the day.

If bike moves are new in your area, you might consider giving back by telling members of the press about the event. Send a story and a link to photos (with permission and attribution) to a few local reporters. If they choose to do a story on your bike move, you might just help inspire others to move by bike, as well.

Be creative about giving back. For my first bike move in 2007, I was really lucky that local zinester and artist Shawn Granton agreed to draw a "Move by Bike" image for the event. I created a silkscreen using Granton's image and prepared a t-shirt silkscreen station at my new house. It was a great souvenir! You could create a postcard pretty easily, as another beyond-the-call thank you.

Perhaps most importantly, give back by helping with other bike moves in the future. Now that you have organized your own move, you understand how important it is to have people show up to help. Be that bike moving rockstar for the next guy's move.

from the canadian ambassador to pedalpalooza
by ron richings

Why I joined my first bike move
To show that it could be done. Fun, fun, fun.

The strangest thing I've moved by bike
Me.

the power of trailers
by mike cobb

Bike trailers are magnificent modules of community empowerment, allowing anybody's favorite and most comfortable bike to become a load-hauler, as needed. When the hauling job is done, the extra "tooling" can be easily removed, restoring the favorite bike to spritely lightweight service. This modularity is so beautiful within the context of a human-powered lifestyle that it must be right. And it's so right that it must be made to proliferate. One trailer can turn a household of bikes into cargo bikes, ON AN AS-NEEDED BASIS. This one trailer can also turn your neighbor's bike into a cargo bike. How perfectly subversive to car culture.

Unfortunately, trailers are sheltered from full societal exploitation by tenacious paradigms.

The first paradigmatic hurdle is the classic: "bikes are toys, not tools of business and basic lifestyle support". If you can soften that one, then another pops up in it's place: "people who haul car loads by bike and trailer are not from my tribe. This crazy activity is best done by athletic activists with fully-developed martyr complexes. Hauling 200 pounds by bike is like hauling 200 pounds without a bike: heroic effort required".

Here lies a piece of my life work: to expose people to the beautiful paradigm-killing truth. Hauling a load by trailer on flat ground is HARDLY ANY DIFFERENT THAN RIDING AN UNLOADED BIKE ON FLAT GROUND. Amazing to most, simple physics to those who've tried.

The four squares of the Knowledge Matrix includes the "knowledge that you don't have and don't know you don't have". Behavior or lack of behavior, driven in part by this ignorance to what CAN be known ends up providing a basic advocacy challenge in any realm. Even many bike activist friends of mine suffer from this uninformed platform of hesitation. A deeply important advocacy mission results.

Dear bike trailer doubter: allow for gentle bike and trailer acceleration on flat terrain and honestly, momentum starts to butter your bread - the trailer "burden" never shows up. Suddenly, the first time trailer hauling experience becomes a rebirth and avoiding car use starts to look utterly reasonable. It's all about getting you to haul that trailer for the first time. Riding is believing.

OK - and what about hills? Hills are harder. We're used to ignoring topography in our life decisions, and cars help us get away with that lack of consideration. Gravity does matter. Before cars, settlements were sculpted by topography: low lands, next to resources, were the only places to live. If we were to maintain such standards, bike trailer-hauling would hardly be affected by routing choices. As it is, if your American city has hills, there might be resources located on top of said hills. This is where routing, patience, and a full range of gears comes in. Can you get what you need and haul it to where it needs to go without climbing? No? Do you have mountain bike-style low gears? Do you have time to go slow? Yes? Then proceed with a little caution and a lot of conviction. Low gears allow you to divide movement into tiny parcels of mincing effort. Divide and conquer those hills if you must, avoid them if you can.

Trailers add capacity to your favorite bike. Any of your favorite bikes. When the task is done, the trailer decouples and you're back to an extremely efficient tool for light load travel, while the trailer can stay busy multiplying the utility and ease of your carfree community. Want less car, more bike in your community? Assign one trailer to every garage or every block or every tool-lending library or all of the above. Low buy-in with high output: an advocate's dream!

delicious

FUEL

cooking for the indeterminate masses
by kristi joy falkowski

Bike moves are awesome to participate in because you get grub and grog and good social hangouts in exchange for just a little work. It is feel-good all the way. If you are hosting, however, you may be thinking, "OH MY GOSH! How many people are coming? How do I know? What do I cook? How much do I cook? What about food allergies/intolerances and preferences? How do I accommodate X? How do I get the food made when I am moving and packing? How do I get it to the new place and heated up?" In short, it can be stressful if you let it be. Sometimes it's stressful anyway. Moving IS. It's ok.

I have hosted three bike moves. Each one taught me a little more. SO I'm going to give you a few pointers and coupla recipes. You can do this.

First, if you post your event on Facebook and invite people, you will get a rough estimate for number of attendees. I add about +5 to the "going" number and plan to make enough to feed that many people. Worse comes to worst and not that many people show? Hey! You just moved! Leftovers! Don't worry about unpacking that kitchen so fast. Too many people come? Well you can plan for that. Hang on, we'll get to how.

How do you get food cooked in time and to the right location when you are packing your kitchen? First you can cook ahead of time. Many recipes can be made a day or more in advance and heated up on site. Crock pots, ovens, Microwaves, stove tops etc. are all excellent reheating devices! Ask to borrow items like a slow cooker. This can be an invaluable tool for reheating foods, because you can put it on low and leave it for…hours. Summer? Make a cold food spread!

Step 1: Make your food in advance, stash the right food at the right location

How do you heat up the food at the end location when you need to start at the start? My advice is to have a friend be your kitchen helper. This person day of event doesn't move stuff, but gets the food set up at the end point. Give 'em a key, show them what needs to be prepped or heated up, etc. and let them help you. This is a great job for that person who wants to help but doesn't have a bike, trailer or says, "If you want me to drive some stuff…" If you truly don't have a person, plan food that heats up quickly, doesn't require cooking; or plan your move so you have time to set crockpots before your move and make it back to your start point.

Step 2: Discover what to cook/make/buy etc.

Once the logistics are set up, and you have a rough estimate of movers, you can plan your meal. You know your limitations; make sure you set a budget for yourself if you need to. This will inform your food choices. Buy or brew coffee for instance? Pizza delivery or homemade chili? Up to you as to how much work/how much money you want to spend. Sometimes, if you have it, spending the money can equal peace of mind. Things to consider: how much you want to spend, how much things will cost, how much you need to make. Pencil it out before you shop.

Step 3: Predict food restrictions

If you know everyone coming, this is easier. If you have unknown helpers, you are going to have to guess. You can ask on your event that people with food restrictions contact you so you can accommodate them, if you want to. It's your move. Ultimately you can serve whatever you like. That said, planning to cook a vegan spread is a good way to go. You have now covered everyone that is vegan, dairy free, vegetarian and omnivorous in one fell swoop. Good job.

If you *know* gluten-free (GF) people are coming, or even just one, have *something* they can eat.

Step 4: Plan your meals

You have the start point and the end point. Start points can be light
snacks and beverages. If it's a morning start, this can be doughnuts,
bagels + toppings (nutella, cream cheese, peanut butter, jelly,
hummus...), fruit, hummus and chips, salsa, etc. Juices, tea, water,
and sparking water are all good drink options. If you brew coffee, you
will want some kind of brew pots or cambros or even an igloo type
water cooler to keep the coffee hot. Ask around to see if anyone has
any you can borrow. You can also buy brewed coffee for a premium
from some coffee shops. Don't forget to supply cups, cream (or soy),
sugar, and hot tea options. Afternoon start? Fruit, chips, pita, hummus,
olives, raw veggies and dips all make great start foods.

Clean up? You probably still need to clean your old place anyway,
right? Pick up/ wrap up a few things? Awesome. You can just leave
everything behind and clean up later. Not the case? You have to be
cleared out that day? Again...find a friend to be your sweep. They can
clean up/pack up all the remaining food fixings and dishes and meet
you at the end point a little after everyone else. Remember to save
them some food!

Step 5: End point

A spread of hors d'ouvres type snacky goods? A pot of something
with a side or two? Mix and match stuff? It all depends on how much
you want to serve and what you feel like making. You can order pizza
- including a few vegan pies and one with a GF crust (if that is an
option at your pizza place) - but that cost adds up fast. I like to make
something that I can stretch if more people show up than I expect,
using ingredients that can be mixed and matched. For the last move,
I made regular and GF pasta with a choice of vegan and GF sauces,
and sides of vegan sausage, meat sausage, and roasted veggies. I could
have extended the sauce if needed with more tomato sauce and veggie
stock. I have also made soups. Soups are GREAT. You can always add
more broth or stock if you need to, and veggie soup is cheap. Include
some bread on the side, some snacks of hummus and chips or dessert
of cookies, and you are good to go. Chili and lentil and bean dishes are
also great for this same reason. They are also dirt cheap to make.

When should you make it? If you have fridge space, cook up to a day or more in advance and store it. Cooking the day of your move is suicide. Prepare in advance.

End point beverages are beer. And wine. And soda or sparking water. Get whatever you want to serve, really. Beer is a crowd-pleaser and few will turn down a PBR if it's all you got, but always have some yummy non-alcoholic options on hand.

Step 6: Stage your food

That's my advice, others may have bits of wisdom of their own to impart. It need not be fancy. Simple fare is delicious. Do not stress about it, people are there to help you. People do like the food, but no matter what you serve, it will be awesome.

Step 7: Remember to breathe!

Now for a couple of my easy recipes. For information, I am a fly-by-the-seat-of-my-pants type of cook. I rarely write anything down, so the following recipes are written to the best of my recollection! Taste as you go.

simple pasta sauce
kristi joy falkowski

INGRESDIENTS
2-28 oz cans tomato sauce
2-28oz diced tomatoes
2 cans tomato paste
1 liter tetra pack Veggie stock or broth
1 cup red wine
Olive oil
1 large yellow onion
4-6 cloves Garlic
1 large Carrot
1 large Green pepper
1 large red pepper
2 tblsp Oregano(fresh)
2-3 inch sprig rosemary (fresh)
2 tsp thyme (fresh)
2 Bay leaves
1 tsp Chili flakes (or to taste you can always leave this out on the table as a condiment!)
Salt to taste
Pepper to taste

TOPPINGS
Parmesan and nutritional yeast flakes (vegan parm!)
feeds 10

To extend sauce **per 5 people**
(Note: this will dilute the herb and veggie flavors concentrated in the original. If you buy tomatoes that are spiced or an Italian style vegan soup, you can alleviate some of that loss.

INGREDIENTS
1 cans tomato sauce
1 can diced tomatoes
½ liter stock
1 cans tomato paste
1 tblsp molasses or brown sugar

Directions

1.   Dice onion, carrot and green+ red peppers, smash the garlic and chop roughly
2.   Place a large stock pot on the stove and pour a tablespoon of olive oil in, heat on medium-high.
3.   Add veggies and sauté (do not burn) until onions are soft and translucent.
4.   Add herbs and let sauté for a couple min with vegetables
5.   Add all tomatoes and stir.
6.   Add wine
7.   Add ¼-3/4 the broth.. You aren't making soup, though water will evaporate off as the sauce simmers. You don't want a soupy sauce.
8.   Taste and salt/pepper to taste
9.   Lower heat to a low simmer
10. Simmer sauce and add more broth if sauce gets to thick. Simmer for 1-3 hours. This is a good slow cooker sauce, longer cooking=better sauce.

potato leek soup (chunky or creamy)
kristi joy falkowski

INGREDIENTS

4 liter tetra packs veggie broth or stock
3 large leeks
4 large waxy potatoes
2 large carrots
2 large celery stocks
2 tsp sage (fresh)
2 tsp thyme (fresh)
2 tsp parsley (flat Italian, fresh)
1-2in spring rosemary (fresh)
4-6 cloves garlic
Olive oil
Salt pepper to taste
For creamy:
2 tetra packs "milk" I prefer So Delicious coconut milk
Nutritional yeast
To extend: have 1-litre box of stock for each 4 more people
¼ dice on carrot, celery and potato

DIRECTIONS

1. Halve and slice leeks thin
2. Crush and roughly chop garlic
3. Mince fresh herbs
4. Place stock pot on stove, medium high heat, 1-2 tblsp olive oil in bottom of pot
5. Add leeks, sauté for 2 -3 min then add diced veg, garlic, sauté till leeks are lightly browning and veg are softening, add fresh herbs, sauté for another min or two, add stock and bring to just a boil, and then turn down to a simmer, salt and pepper to taste, cook until potatoes are just tender.

For creamy + chunky add 2-3 cups "milk" and some earth balance margarine or other vegan margarine and about 1 tbsp nutritional yeast

For creamy and smooth, replace 1 liter broth\with 1 liter milk, cook the veggies longer until very soft, then use a blender or immersion blender to puree, strain through a sieve if you want to get chunks left over out. Add "butter".

feeds 10

bike move vegan cincinnati-style chili
or
how to feed delicious food to 20 hungry people with 8 different food needs in one crockpot
lily karabaic

INGREDIENTS

3 cups dry black beans
2 cups dry chili or kidney beans
2 cans diced tomatoes with chilis
1 small can of chilis in adobo sauce
3 carrots
1 large onion (not sweet)
7 cloves garlic, minced
2 habenero peppers
7 jalapenos
4 serranos sliced
1 yellow bell pepper,
1 red bell pepper
Optional: 1 bag of smart ground or some other frozen vegan TVP-esque thing (I like Morningstar Farms Grillers Burger Style Recipe Crumbles but they aren't gluten-free)
lil bit cilantro
lil bit olive oil
cumin
paprika
chili powder
garlic powder
onion powder
tiny tiny bit of powdered cocoa

DIRECTIONS

1. Rinse beans and soak in twice as much water as there is beans for 5-6 hours.
2. Drain, rinse and fill with water enough to cover beans.
3. Chop cilantro, peppers, onions, garlic, and the chilis in adobo.
4. Sautee the onions and garlic first, mix in the spices and cocoa as the onions become translucent.

5. Add everything to one big crockpot (including the fake meat things if you have it)!

Depending on your time frame, put in a crock pot and set temperature to high and cook for 3-4 hours. Or cook on low for 6-8 hours. Or cook on low for 6-8 hours, and "warm" until serving. Before serving, take 4 cups of the chili out of the crockpot, liquidize in a blender and mix back up. That's what makes it cincinnati-style chili! And delicious.

Serve with: salsa, tortilla chips, sour cream, cheese (I like vegan and non-vegan cheese), shredded lettuce, fresh scallions, and possibly macaroni (if you're from the part of the country that does chilimac). Macaroni can be cooked ahead, stored in the fridge, and served cold (the heat of the chili will warm it up.) If yr real ambitious, mix up a batch of cornbread and cook it the night before.

Yum, yum, yum. This recipe is vegan, can be made gluten-free without the fake meatz, all sortz of them other food needs. Eat it up and congratulate yourself for a great bike move!

slow cooker lentil soup
esther harlow

Vegan! Hot on cold winter days! You can set it & forget it night before. Only catch: slow cooker must be still hot when you arrive. (Most turn off automatically after x # of hours.) So make sure it will still be on when the posse arrives, either by having a housemate reset it day-of or having a long enough slow cook.

INGREDIENTS
2 c brown or green lentils (NOT red or orange)
1 box veggie broth
3 c water
3 carrots, chopped
2 celery stalks, chopped
1 onion, chopped
2 garlic cloves
1/2 tsp oregano or italian seasoning
Liberal sprinkle of black pepper
1 tsp salt
1 can diced tomatoes :3 tbl olive oil

DIRECTIONS
1. Put all ingredients in a slow cooker.
2. Cook for 12 hours.

Double or triple depending on how big your slow cooker is.

Make sure to have some loaves of crusty bread to eat with it, and unsweetened yogurt (vegan & non) to dollop on top in the bowl & swirl in- makes it nice and rich.

yummy pasta salad
esther harlow

For summer. Cook day before at new house and leave in fridge there.

Short cut pasta (I like rigatoni, penne or penne rigate - around 1 lb:5 ppl)
Handful of basil, chopped
A few oz kalamata olives, sliced
A couple colorful tomatoes, chopped
Minced garlic
Olive oil
Balsamic vinegar
Salt
Pepper

1. Cook the pasta day before.
2. Drain the pasta while it's still a bit chewy
3. Saute the minced garlic in a healthy dollop of olive oil, just so it turns golden.
4. Mix together the pasta & garlic olive oil in a large bowl.
5. Add the rest of the olives & veggies, while the pasta's still hot.

Make sure there's enough olive oil and balsamic vinegar to make everything yummy (requires frequent tasting), salt & pepper to taste. Refrigerate covered.

You can substitute or add to the tomatoes with whatever's in season. June: snap peas (blanched in hot water if they have tough skins), broccoli sliced (again, blanched if it's not tender); July, August, September: corn scraped off the cob, beans (blanched), peppers (sauted with the olive oil, or roasted); summer squash (also sauted); cherry tomatoes instead of chopped tomatoes; have fresh mozzarella chopped for the dairy-eaters, drained cannelini beans for everyone, as optional protein.

quinoa apple spice cake
kristin bott

(adapted from http://foodieunderground.com/quinoa-apple-spice-cake) Hat tip to Anna Brones

INGREDIENTS
1 cup uncooked quinoa or a mixture of quinoa and millet
1 cup buckwheat flour (ground kasha)
1 large apple (or as many small apples), diced or shredded
3 eggs
8 tablespoons coconut oil, melted
1 teaspoon baking powder
1 teaspoon baking soda
1 teaspoon sea salt
1/2 cup while sugar
1 teaspoon cinnamon
1 teaspoon ginger (or more, grated fresh = my favorite)
1/2 teaspoon nutmeg
1 teaspoon vanilla extract
shredded coconut (optional)

This is the recipe that you hand to your friends who want to help and have a ton of time but can't make it on the day. Or who aren't able to ride. Or or or or or. I'd recommend against making this if you're moving – only because it's not a one-step process. Strongly recommended if you have gluten free folks showing up – or if you have people who want something protein-intense. This is not vegan! I am sorry. You can add all sorts of things, chunks of candied ginger or chopped nuts or or or – go nuts. Let your bikey move helpers be inspired.

DIRECTIONS

1. Cook quinoa or quinoa/millet mixture. (2 c water at a boil + 1 c raw grain + dash of salt.

2. Let simmer 12-15 minutes or until water is gone.)

3. Mix together everything dry (note: quinoa is "wet").

4. Whisk together coconut oil and eggs, add to dry.

5. Combine quinoa and apple bits.

6. Throw everything together.

7. Grease a pan of choice (9" baking, I'm partial to bundts). Put shredded coconut on the bottom if you'd like – or on the top if you'd prefer.

8. Pour batter into pan.

9. Bake at 350 for 30-40 until it passes toothpick test

pfeffernusse
kristin bott

INGREDIENTS

1 1/2 cup flour of your choosing
1/2 cup almond meal (or silvered almonds, ground in coffee grinder/mashed with a rolling pin or hammer or...)
1/2 teaspoon salt of any kind (sea, lake, slough, iodized, kosher...)
1 teaspoon each: anise, cinnamon, cardamom
1/2 teaspoon each: allspice, nutmeg, cloves, black pepper
1/2 cup coconut oil
1/2 cup molasses
1/2 cup brown sugar
Powdered sugar

DIRECTIONS

1. Combine flour, almond meal, salt, and spices. (If using whole spices, throw in coffee grinder or morter and pestle if you're into that.)
2. In a separate container, melt coconut oil and blend in molasses and brown sugar.
3. Combine the two mixtures and refrigerate two hours or overnight or skip that step entirely because you're moving and you have shit to do!
4. Separate dough into small chunks (about 2 tablespoons) and roll into balls.
5. Bake on ungreased sheets at 350F for 7-10 minutes.
6. When cool enough to handle but still warm, roll cookies in powdered sugar. (The sugar will stick best to warm cookies.)
7. Store in an airtight container for up to six months.

These freeze really well; feel free to bake and freeze before you pack. Label as vegan and grab all of the vegans you know and make sure they get some.

deena's chewy chocolate chip cookies
kristin bott

(http://mostlyfoodstuffs.blogspot.com/2009/08/chewy-chocolate-chocolate-chip-cookies.html) Hat tip to Deena Prichep; hat tip to Post Punk Kitchen

INGREDIENTS

4 tsp flaxseed meal (or grind yr own flaxseeds in a coffee grinder)
1/2 cup nut-milk or soymilk
2 cups flour of your choosing
1 cup cocoa powder
1 tsp baking soda
3/4 tsp salt
3/4 cup neutral oil (olive oil works but has a taste, grapeseed or sunflower or canola can work too)
2 cups sugar (half brown sugar if you want)
2 tsp vanilla
1 cup chocolate chips
optional: nuts to taste (1/2 c chopped walnuts or pecans)

DIRECTIONS

1. Preheat oven at 350.
2. Whisk together flaxseeds and milk and let sit for a half-hour or so. This is not a joke. For serious and for reals, a half-hour. Quoth Deena, who knows things about food.
    (IMPORTANT: this allows the flax seeds to release whatever it is they release into the milk, which binds the cookies into a nice chewy consistency. If they don't sit long enough, you'll have disappointingly flat cookies).
3. Find a bowl you haven't packed. Mix: flour, cocoa powder, baking soda, salt.
4. Find another bowl you haven't packed. Whisk: oil, sugar, vanilla, flax+milk mixture. Mix well.
5. Fold together: wet + dry, don't overmix. Add chocolate chips and optional nuts.

6. Make the smallest size cookies you think are reasonable (this is a bike move, people – everyone is hungry and you have to Feed The People) – about 1" spheres work well.

7. Place on ungreased cookie sheet or baking pan or anything else that isn't in a box already. Leave 1" between cookies.

8. Bake 8-10 minutes - do not bake more than 10 minutes.

9. Allow cookies to set a bit before moving to a cooling rack.

Feed to vegans and non-vegans.

acknowledgments

Moving by bike is not possible without a supportive community. It is difficult to properly express my gratitude and impossible to name everyone who should be thanked for making this zine come to life.

Shift is a loose association of bike funnists that has been making the Portland, Oregon metropolitan region a more vibrant place to bike in and enjoy since 2002. Through an online listserve and calendar, Shift promotes such bastions of bike fun as Moving by Bike, Breakfast on the Bridges, Pedalpalooza, and the World Naked Bike Ride. Most of the amazing contributors in this zine are actively involved in Shift. Thanks to all who have joined a bike move, shared their stories, and/or furthered bike fun.

Find Shift: www.shift2bikes.org

The Independent Publishing Resource Center allowed this zine idea to meet the page. Special thanks to the instructors and participants of the 2012-2013 Fiction/Creative Nonfiction Certificate Program, who have been guides and inspirations.

Find the IPRC: www.iprc.org

The Portland Society is a nonprofit business alliance of professional women who are passionate about bicycling in Portland, Oregon. Portland Society members believed in this project enough to choose me as the recipient of the 2012 Portland Society Fund grant. Thank you all.

Find the Portland Society: www.portlandsociety.org